CAN'T I JUST HIT RESET?

A Book About Making Mistakes and Being Okay Anyway

Jennifer Larsen

Originality Statement

This book is an original work written by the author and reflects their unique ideas, voice, and instructional approach. While it may reference common educational and career-planning concepts, all content, including structure, language, exercises, and framework, is the author's own creation. Any similarities to other published works are purely coincidental.

Printed in the United States of America

ISBN: 978-1-968756-97-0

First Edition

Cover design by Rachel Bostwick

Interior design and layout by Rachel Bostwick

For information or bulk orders, visit cantijust.com

CAN'T I JUST HIT RESET?

A BOOK ABOUT MAKING MISTAKES AND BEING OKAY ANYWAY

INTRO:
WELCOME TO THE GAME

Have you ever done something that made your stomach drop?

Like, right after it happened, you wanted to disappear... or rewind time... or suddenly develop the ability to shrink down and live in your sock drawer forever?

Yeah. You're not alone.

Everyone messes up. Seriously – **everyone**. Kids, adults, teachers, even the characters in your favorite games.

We forget things.

We lose our temper.

We say the wrong thing, or nothing at all.

Sometimes we make a mistake that hurts someone we care about – and then we feel terrible.

That's what this book is about.

Not about being perfect. Not about getting every moment right.

It's about what happens **after** the mess-up.

What you think. What you feel. What you do next.

And – most importantly – **how you treat yourself** when you know you made a mistake.

Think of this book like a game.

Not one with dragons or lasers (sorry), but one where **you're the main player** and each chapter is a new level.

Some levels are easy. Some are hard. Some will feel like boss fights with your own brain.

And that's okay — because... this game?

You don't have to beat it all at once. You don't have to be fast or perfect. You just have to keep playing.

There's no "Game Over" here. Just **checkpoints, power-ups,** and a chance to get stronger every time you hit reset.

✏️ How this book works:

- Each chapter = one emotional level to work through

- You'll read some ideas, try an activity, and get a little "lunchbox note" at the end – a short message meant to help you feel braver and kinder toward yourself

- You can go in order, or skip around if you want. This is *your* game.

Let's start at Level 1:

You messed up.

Now what?

(You're gonna be okay, I promise.)

LEVEL 1:

OOPS!–
WHEN YOU MAKE A MISTAKE

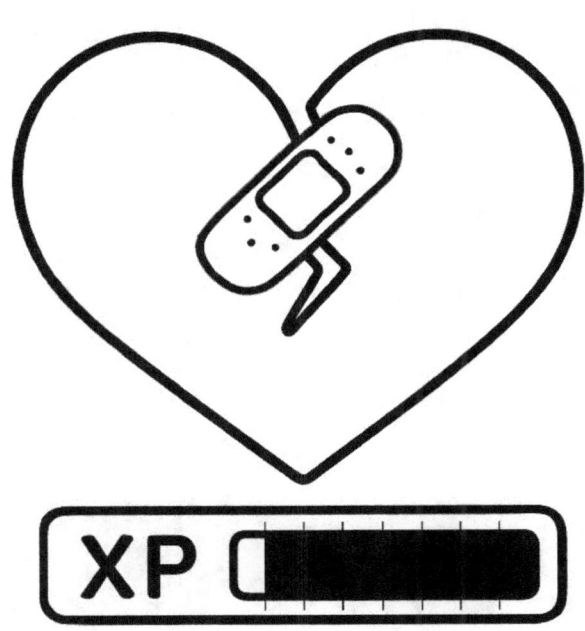

Let's just get this out of the way: **you're going to mess up.** Not once. Not twice. A whole bunch of times. You probably already have.

And that's not because you're bad or broken or lazy.

It's because you're a human. And humans do stuff. And when people do stuff, they **sometimes do it wrong**.

Maybe you forgot something important.

Maybe you broke a rule or someone's trust.

Maybe you told a lie because the truth was too scary.

Maybe you snapped at someone, or hurt them by accident.

Maybe you did something you *knew* wasn't okay, and now your stomach hurts just thinking about it.

Whatever your version of "oops" is, here's what I want you to know:

You're still okay.

A mistake is something you *did*, not something you *are.*

⚠ But It Still Feels Bad...

Of course it does. Nobody *likes* messing up. When you're a good person – and yes, I believe you are – your brain and heart **care** when you hurt someone or do something wrong.

That feeling in your chest? That twist in your belly? That's your conscience. It means you *care*. And that's actually a good thing.

But we don't want to live in that feeling forever, right? We want to learn from it and move on.

So let's talk about that.

💬 Learning from Oopses (Yes, that's a word now)

Think about a video game character walking right off a cliff.

They fall.

Splat.

Next time? They jump sooner.

That's how we grow.

Every time you mess up – and you will – you get a chance to:

- Notice what went wrong
- Understand why it happened
- Try something better next time

That's not failure. That's leveling up.

✂ Activity: The Mistake Map

Let's turn your oops into something useful.

Take a piece of paper and draw a simple map – boxes, arrows, or just a list is fine.

Pick a mistake you've made recently. Write it down. Then think through what happened next.

What did you learn from it?

What would you do differently next time?

What happened after?

Here's an example:

Oops: I yelled at my sister.

Then: I got in trouble and felt bad.

Learned: I yell when I'm already tired or frustrated.

Next time: I'll take a break before answering when I feel that way.

Now: We're okay again, and I'm working on it.

You don't have to show your map to anyone. It's just for you. A way to **see that one mistake is not the whole story.** It's just a moment on the path.

THE MISTAKE MAP

Oops: I yelled at my sister.

↓

Then: I got in trouble and felt bad

↓

Learned: I yell when I'm already tired or frustrated

↓

Now: We're okay again, and I'm working on it.

 ## LUNCHBOX NOTE:

Even when you drop the ball, I'm still cheering for you.

LEVEL 2:

THE GLITCH GREMLIN – FEELING ASHAMED OR STUCK

Sometimes after a mistake, something worse shows up.

Not a grown-up. Not even consequences.

Just this... feeling.

Heavy. Icky. Quiet. Loud. All at once.

You want to hide.

You want to go back in time.

You want to *not be the person who did that thing*.

That feeling? It has a name.

It's called **shame**.

And wow, is it sticky.

Meet the Glitch Gremlin

If shame were a video game character, it'd be a glitch gremlin.

It pops up when things go wrong. It tells you the worst things about yourself.

It says stuff like:

"Everyone saw that."

"You ruined everything."

"You're the bad guy now."

And worst of all?

"You don't deserve to feel better."

Yikes.

Let's be clear: **that gremlin lies**.

It shows up when you feel embarrassed, guilty, or stuck... and then it starts building a nest in your brain.

But here's the truth:

You can notice the gremlin without believing it.

☼ Getting Unstuck

When you're stuck in shame, you might:

- Replay the mistake over and over
- Avoid people or hide
- Get angry to cover up the guilt
- Say mean things to yourself in your head

But guess what? That doesn't fix anything.

It just keeps the gremlin well-fed.

What *does* help?

- Talking to someone kind
- Saying what happened out loud
- Letting yourself feel bad for a minute – **and then move on**
- Reminding yourself that good people make bad choices some-times

You don't have to carry shame like it's part of your identity. It's not. It's just **a feeling passing through**.

✂ Activity: Name the Gremlin

Let's draw this shame creature and take away some of its power.

On a blank page:

- Draw what your Glitch Gremlin looks like. Is it furry? Slimy? Wearing socks?

- What does it say to you when you mess up?

- Now write (or draw) what *you* want to say back.

Example:

> *"You're right, I did mess up...*
>
> *but I'm still a good kid, and I'm working on it.*
>
> *You don't get to decide who I am."*

You just talked back to shame. That's a big win.

LUNCHBOX NOTE:

LEVEL 3:

THE APOLOGY QUEST – HOW TO MAKE THINGS RIGHT

You messed up. You feel it. Maybe even talked back to your Glitch Gremlin.

Now what?

Well... sometimes, the next step is facing the other person.

And yeah – it can feel like a **boss battle.**

Apologizing is one of the hardest and most important things you can do.

It takes guts, kindness, and honesty. But when you do it right, it can also be **one of the most powerful healing tools you'll ever unlock.**

Let's break it down.

What a Real Apology Looks Like

A real apology isn't just saying "I'm sorry" fast so you don't get in trouble.

A real apology means:

- **You understand what you did**

- **You care how it affected the other person**

- **You're trying to make things better**

Here's a simple recipe:

1. Say what happened

"I took your book without asking."

2. Say how you think it made them feel

"I know that probably made you feel disrespected."

3. Say what you're going to do about it

"I won't do that again, and if something goes missing, I'll help look."

You don't need to give a big speech or cry or beat yourself up.

You just need to be honest, even if it's awkward.

⚠ **What Not to Do**

✖ "Sorry if you felt bad."

(That's not an apology. That's a dodge.)

✖ "I said I was sorry, okay?!"

(That's anger trying to cover up guilt.)

✖ "You're too sensitive."

(That's making it their fault.)

If you're not ready to apologize yet, take a little space – but **don't wait forever**. The longer you wait, the heavier it feels.

And once you do it? It's like **clearing a stage**. Yo.

🛠 Activity: Fix-It Toolkit

Let's make a list of tools you can use to make things better after a mistake.

Some examples:

- Saying something kind

- Writing a short note or text

- Drawing a picture

- Helping with something the person needs

- Giving space but checking back in later

Now write or draw your own "Fix-It Toolkit."

Keep it simple. This is just a reminder that you have options.

If someone pops into your head while you're doing this... maybe today's the day to use a tool.

📝 LUNCHBOX NOTE:

Saying sorry doesn't make you weak—it makes you brave.

LEVEL 4:

CHECKPOINT! – GIVING YOURSELF A SECOND CHANCE

In a lot of games, there's something called a **checkpoint.**

It's the spot the game sends you back to when things go wrong.

You mess up. You fall. You lose.

Then – **pop!** – you're back at your last checkpoint, ready to try again.

Life works like that too.

Not always perfectly. Not always immediately. But most of the time, you get **another shot**.

You just have to allow yourself to **start over**.

🔄 Why It's Hard to Hit Reset

Sometimes, we keep replaying a mistake in our heads because we think we *deserve* to feel bad.

We think:

"I shouldn't move on yet."

"If I feel better, it means I didn't care."

"I should stay mad at myself."

But guess what?

Feeling bad forever doesn't fix anything.

And it doesn't prove you're good, either.

What proves you're a good person is learning, growing, and **giving yourself the same kindness you'd give a friend.**

If your best friend messed up and felt terrible, would you tell them to stay stuck and miserable?

Or would you help them hit restart?

Be that kind to *you*, too.

Permission to Try Again

Even if the situation didn't magically fix itself...

Even if the person you hurt still needs time...

Even if you're still disappointed in yourself...

You are allowed to try again.

Try to do better.

Try to speak kindly.

Try to believe you're still good and worthy.

That's your checkpoint moment.

You've learned something.

You're still here.

And you get to go forward.

⚒ Activity: Respawn Routine

Let's build your personal reset plan.

RESPAWN STATION

- Deep breath
- Going outside
- Saying "I forgive myself"
- Drawing or writing
- Talking to someone
- Hugging a pet or plushie
- Listening to music

What helps you feel ready to try again?

Here are some ideas:

- Deep breath

- Going outside

- Saying "I forgive myself" out loud

- Drawing or writing

- Talking to someone you trust

- Hugging a pet or plushie

- Listening to music

Now make your list – or draw your "respawn station."

It's your checkpoint. Visit it anytime you need to come back to yourself.

LUNCHBOX NOTE:

You're allowed
to try again.
You're allowed
to be new today.

 # LEVEL 5:

SPECTATOR MODE -
WHAT YOU THINK OTHERS SEE

Ever had a moment where you thought,

"Everyone saw that"?

"Now they all think I'm awful"?

"I can never show my face again"?

Welcome to **Spectator Mode** – that weird part of your brain that makes you feel like you're on stage, and the whole world is watching your every move.

The truth?

Most of them didn't see it.

Some of them saw but forgot already.

And the ones who *did* remember? They've messed up too.

🧠 Everyone's Busy Being Themselves

Think about the last time someone else messed up – tripped, said the wrong word, spilled something.

Did you judge them forever?

Or did you just think, "Oops," and move on?

People are mostly wrapped up in their own worries.

They're wondering things like:

"Did I wear the wrong shirt today?"

"Did I say something weird?"

"Does everyone think I'm annoying?"

In other words: **they're not thinking about you as much as you think they are.**

That doesn't mean they don't care about you – it just means they're not focused on your every move.

And that's actually good news.

Because it means you can **mess up, repair it, and keep going** without the whole world freezing in judgment.

😶 But What If They Are Judging Me?

Okay, real talk? Sometimes people are unkind. Sometimes someone *does* laugh or roll their eyes or say something that makes it worse.

That sucks.

But that doesn't mean you deserve it.

And it doesn't mean their opinion is the truth.

You are allowed to mess up and still be liked.

You are allowed to grow and get better and not be trapped in that one moment forever.

No one else gets to freeze you in time and say, "That's who you are now."

Not even you.

✂ Activity: The Crowd's Not Watching

Let's draw a moment where you felt embarrassed. Something recent or something that still pops into your head.

Now – draw the people around you. But this time, draw *what they were actually thinking*.

Maybe one was worried about their test.

One was thinking about lunch.

One was playing a video in their head from two days ago.

Maybe one was quietly rooting for you to be okay.

You are not the center of everyone's thoughts.
And that's a **huge relief.**

 LUNCHBOX NOTE:

LEVEL 6:

THE INVENTORY CHECK – GOOD THINGS ABOUT YOU

Let's say you're in a game. You've been through a few rough levels.

You fought off the shame gremlin, battled through an apology, survived a social slip-up...

Before you go any further, it's time to check your inventory.

What are you carrying with you?

When we mess up, our brains sometimes shrink everything down to one thing:

"I'm the kid who yelled."

"I'm the one who broke the rule."

"I'm the person who ruined that moment."

But you are **so much more** than your worst moments.

You're also:

- The friend who shared your snack

- The kid who helped someone find their lost pencil

- The person who made someone laugh when they really needed it

The good stuff doesn't disappear when something goes wrong.

You're still you — even if your character tripped on a lava block five minutes ago.

💬 Rebalancing the Scoreboard

Mess-ups feel *loud*. They take up a lot of space in our heads.

That's why it's important to **name the good stuff on purpose** – to remind yourself that you're still doing your best, and that effort counts.

You might not notice your kindness, your effort, or your thoughtfulness in the moment – but it's all in your inventory. It's there.

Let's go find it.

✂ Activity: Backpack of Strengths

Draw a backpack. Big or small. Your dream pack. Whatever you like.

Now, imagine you're going on a journey and you can only bring the **emotional tools and traits you already have**.

What goes in the bag?

BACKPACK OF STRENGTHS

FLASHLIGHT OF HONESTY · HOODIE OF KINDNESS · NOTE BOOK · SHIELD OF EFFORT · WATER BOTTLE OF FORGIVENESS

Here are some ideas:

- A flashlight of honesty

- A hoodie of kindness

- A notebook of creativity

- A shield of effort

- A compass of fairness

- A water bottle of forgiveness

Add your own. Make it yours.
You've earned more gear than you realize.

LUNCHBOX NOTE:

Don't forget the awesome things you already have equipped

 # LEVEL 7

THE FINAL BOSS – FORGIVING YOURSELF

Okay, you've made it through the levels.

You looked at the mistake. Faced the shame gremlin. Talked to some-one. Hit restart. Noticed the people around you. Remembered the good things you carry.

Now it's time for the **final level**.

The one where you look yourself in the mirror (or your reflection in the toaster) and say:

"I forgive you."

Even if the mistake wasn't fixed yet.

Even if someone's still upset.

Even if the memory pops back sometimes.

You still get to forgive yourself.

⚔ Why This Boss Is So Hard

Some people think forgiving yourself means you didn't care.

Or that you're pretending nothing happened.

Or that you don't feel bad anymore.

But that's not what forgiveness is.

Forgiving yourself just means:

- You've faced what happened
- You're trying to grow from it
- And you're ready to stop treating yourself like a villain

You don't have to punish yourself forever to prove you're good.

You're already good.

And you're getting better all the time.

What Forgiveness Sounds Like

It doesn't have to be a big speech.

You don't need permission from anyone else.

You can say it out loud.

You can whisper it.

You can write it down.

You can think it and mean it.

"I messed up, but I'm still trying."

"I was wrong, and I want to do better."

"I forgive myself, even if I still feel a little bad."

"I'm not perfect. I'm learning."

That's enough.

✂ Activity: Write a Forgiveness Code

A lot of games have special codes or buttons you press to unlock something.

Let's make your forgiveness code.

FORGIVENESS — CODE —

I made a mistake, but I'm still a good person. I can grow from this.

Write a short sentence or two that you can use whenever you're stuck in guilt or shame.

Here's one:

"I made a mistake, but I'm still a good person. I can grow from this."

Write your version.

Decorate it like a scroll, a badge, a login screen – whatever feels right.

Put it somewhere you can see when you need it.

Because you *will* need it again. And now you'll be ready.

 **LUNCHBOX NOTE:**

You're allowed
to move on,
even if it still
stings a little.

YOU WIN
BY BEING YOU

XP

You've made it through every level.

And no, this doesn't mean you'll never make another mistake.

It doesn't mean you'll never feel bad again, or get stuck, or fall into a new boss fight with your own brain.

But now?

Now you have tools.

You've got a map.

You've got a backpack full of good things.

You've got restart buttons, and check-in points, and lunchbox notes tucked in your memory.

And best of all?

You know that messing up doesn't make you unworthy.

It just makes you human.

The real goal here was never perfection.

The goal was to learn how to:

- Face the mess

- Be honest about it

- Make it better when you can

- Be kind to yourself either way

If you can do that? You're already winning.

YOU WON THE GAME !!

And even on the days when you feel like you're not —

You're still good.

You're still growing.

You still matter.

You don't have to be the best player.

You don't have to finish every level perfectly.

You just have to keep showing up and doing your best with the tools you have.

And maybe, as you get stronger, you'll help someone else when *they* hit a glitch.

That's how this game really works.

FINAL LUNCHBOX NOTE:

You're not here to be perfect. You're here to grow. And I love who you're becoming.

✦ Note to Adults

Hi there –

If you're reading this, it likely means you care about a child who is learning how to manage mistakes, big feelings, and the sometimes complicated process of self-forgiveness.

This book was written with their voice in mind – but your voice matters too.

Forgiveness is a hard thing to teach, especially when the world around us pushes perfection, performance, or punishment. Kids pick up on that. They often hold onto guilt longer than we realize, and they're not always sure how to talk about it.

So here's how you can help:

- Be gentle when they mess up – even if there's a consequence

- Model forgiveness out loud ("That really frustrated me... but I forgive you, and I still love you.")

- Let them hear you forgive yourself sometimes, too

- Remind them that mistakes are part of learning, not proof they're a bad person

- Leave room for quiet processing – sometimes they don't need a lecture, just space

Kids don't need to be rescued from every mistake.

But they do need someone who reminds them they are still good, still worthy, and still loved – even when they fall short.

Thank you for being that person.

You're a critical part of their "respawn" routine.

Thanks for showing up.

If this book helped you or your child, there's more where it came from.

The *Can't I Just...* series includes books for every age and stage – helping kids, teens, and adults build confidence, find direction, and feel less alone.

Related Books You Might Like:

- *Can't I Just Be Like Everyone Else?* – Soft skills for teens
- *Can't I Just Stay in My Room?* – Career guide for teens who hate talking about it
- *Can't I Just Skip College?* – Alternatives to traditional college paths
- *Can't I Just Help My Kid Pick a Path?* – A guide for parents navigating career and college decisions

And more are coming soon!

About Wayfinder Foundation Inc.

This book is part of a nonprofit mission.

Wayfinder Foundation Inc. provides educational tools, resources, and programming to help youth and adults explore careers, build life skills, and improve emotional resilience. We believe everyone deserves support, no matter their path.

To learn more or support our mission, visit:

WayfinderFoundationInc.org